NO LONGER PROPERTY OF
ANYTHINK LIBRARIES
RANGEVIEW LIBRARY DISTRICT

anythink

ALTERNATOR
BOOKS™

SPACE IN ACTION

STARS AND GALAXIES IN ACTION

An AUGMENTED REALITY Experience

Rebecca E. Hirsch

Lerner Publications ◆ Minneapolis

EXPLORE SPACE IN BRAND-NEW WAYS WITH AUGMENTED REALITY!

1. Ask a parent or guardian for permission to download the free Lerner AR app on your digital device by going to the App Store or Google Play.

2. As you read, look for this icon throughout the book. It means there is an augmented reality experience on that page!

3. Use the Lerner AR app to scan the picture near the icon.

4. Watch space come alive with augmented reality!

The Apple logo is a trademark of Apple Inc., registered in the U.S. and other countries and regions. App Store is a service mark of Apple Inc. Google Play and the Google Play logo are trademarks of Google LLC.

CONTENTS

INTRODUCTION

STAR POWER

The surface of the sun churns and bubbles. Red-hot gases stream upward in twisting, glowing arcs. They rise hundreds of thousands of miles. More gases swirl in scorching cyclones.

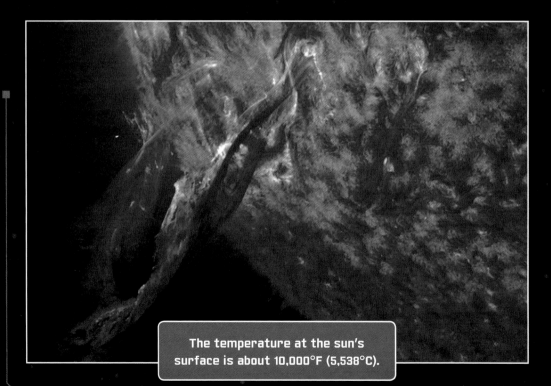

The temperature at the sun's surface is about 10,000°F (5,538°C).

The Milky Way is shaped like a spiral. Everything in the galaxy orbits a black hole at its center.

Earth **orbits** the sun, our nearest star. It is 93 million miles (150 million km) from Earth. If the sun were hollow, 1.3 million Earths could fit inside.

Our sun is a medium-size star. It looks bigger than other stars because it is so close to us. Billions of stars, bigger and smaller than the sun, are scattered across our galaxy, the Milky Way. Billions of galaxies, in all shapes and sizes, are scattered throughout the universe.

THE SUN

NASA's Parker Solar Probe lifted off from Earth in 2018 on a mission to the sun. The probe reached the sun's upper **atmosphere** and sailed through the glowing hot gases. Protected by a high-tech heat shield, it is the first spacecraft to touch a star.

The Parker Solar Probe took this image of the sun's atmosphere in December 2018. The bright dot near the center is the planet Mercury.

Parker Solar Probe

The Parker Solar Probe's heat shield and a cutting-edge cooling system will protect the machine for as long as possible as it gets closer and closer to the sun.

INSIDE THE SUN

Our sun, like all stars, is a glowing ball of hot gases. The source of its light and heat is deep in the center of the sun. In the core, hydrogen **atoms** combine. This process releases huge amounts of energy. The temperature at the core is about 27 million °F (15 million °C).

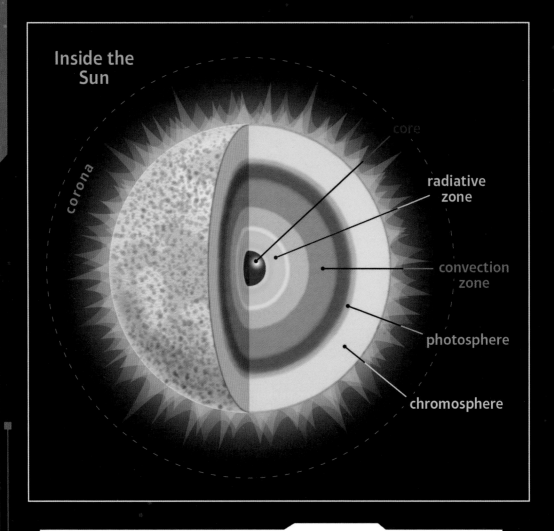

Inside the Sun

core

corona

radiative zone

convection zone

photosphere

chromosphere

As energy travels outward from the core, it passes through two layers, the radiative zone and the convection zone. As it moves, thick, dense gases slow the energy down. It takes about 170,000 years for energy from the core to reach the top of the convection zone.

THE SURFACE OF THE SUN

The outer layer of the sun, the photosphere, is the part we can see. It is a layer of hot, bubbling gases. Although much cooler than the core, the photosphere is still hot enough to boil diamonds.

The sun is surrounded by a scorching hot atmosphere. It is made of two layers, the chromosphere and the corona. Both are hotter than the sun's surface. The temperature of the chromosphere can reach 1.8 million °F (1 million °C). The corona is even hotter at about 3.5 million °F (1.9 million °C). Why the sun's atmosphere is hotter than its surface is a mystery.

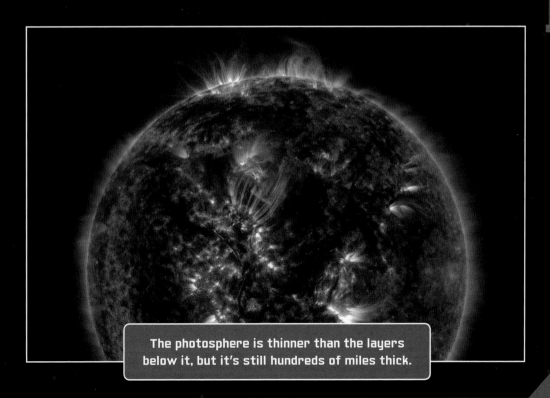

The photosphere is thinner than the layers below it, but it's still hundreds of miles thick.

The sun's surface is never still. Dark areas called sunspots appear on the surface. Sunspots may lead to powerful eruptions that fling streams of **charged particles** and energy into the solar system. Some of these streams reach Earth.

Charged particles from the sun can affect our weather. They may trigger **auroras**, dazzling light shows that are visible near Earth's North Pole and South Pole. Particles can cripple electronic communications and cause power outages on Earth.

Sunspots are cooler than the rest of the photosphere.

Astronomers study the sun more closely than other stars because it is so close to Earth. The Parker Solar Probe is studying the sun's atmosphere and activity. Scientists hope the data it collects will help explain mysteries of the sun such as why the corona is so hot.

Auroras are called northern lights or southern lights depending on where they appear.

THE BIRTH OF STARS

Stars are born in an enormous swirl of gas and dust called a nebula. Gas and dust are the building blocks of new stars. A nebula is cold and scattered across vast distances. A star begins to form when gravity pulls together a clump of a nebula's material.

The Crab Nebula is about 6,500 light-years from Earth. New stars will form from the nebula's gas and dust.

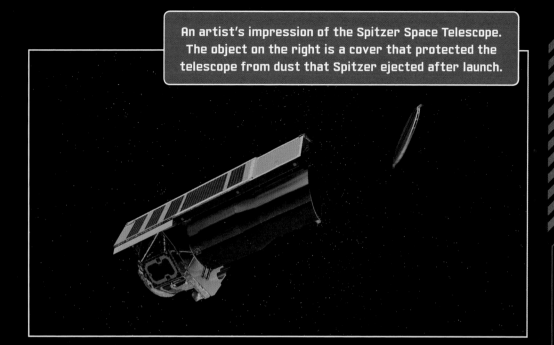

An artist's impression of the Spitzer Space Telescope. The object on the right is a cover that protected the telescope from dust that Spitzer ejected after launch.

As the clump grows, its gravity gets stronger. The dust and gas become tightly packed, causing the clump to grow hotter. Hydrogen atoms begin **fusion**, combining to form heavier atoms such as helium. This process releases heat and light. Eventually, a **chain reaction** starts, with more and more atoms undergoing fusion. The star begins to shine.

Astronomers use NASA's Spitzer Space Telescope and Hubble Space Telescope to study the birth of stars. In 2018 astronomers reported the birth of two new stars in one nebula. Later, they published a photo of the Butterfly Nebula, nicknamed for its shape. The nebula's two butterfly wings are giant bubbles of gas and the birthplace of hundreds of new stars.

THE BURNING OF A STAR

Astronomers classify stars by their size, or **mass**. Supermassive stars are about two hundred times bigger than the sun. They burn hot and blue. Medium-size stars, like our sun, burn cooler and are white, yellow, or orange. Our sun is a yellow dwarf star. The smallest stars, called red dwarfs, are about one-tenth the mass of our sun.

TRAPPIST-1

Sun

This illustration compares the size of the sun to TRAPPIST-1, an ultracool red dwarf.

A star can maintain the balance
between its gravity and its energy
output for billions of years.

A star's life is a struggle between two forces. Gravity pulls inward and threatens to collapse the star. But as long as fusion continues in its core, it remains hot, pushing heat outward. When the heat and gravity are in balance, the star remains stable.

CHAPTER 3

THE DEATH OF STARS

In 2016 light from a giant, exploding star reached Earth. Astronomers around the world turned their telescopes to watch as the distant star died in a violent blast. The explosion of a supermassive star is a **supernova**. It is the largest known explosion in space. It happens when a star runs out of hydrogen and fusion ends. Deep inside the star, gravity takes over and crushes the core.

Scientists used multiple images from the Hubble Space Telescope to create this picture of gas and dust clouds blown into space by a supernova.

Supernova

When a supermassive star explodes, it emits an incredible amount of light and energy.

Charged particles in the core become so tightly packed that they repel one another and the star blows apart.

A supernova blasts gas and dust outward. This glowing cloud can become the birthplace of new stars. Usually the explosion leaves behind a dense core of iron and other elements that can become a **black hole**, the densest known object in the universe.

WHITE DWARFS

Medium-size stars die more peaceful deaths. When a yellow or red dwarf runs out of fuel, the outer layers of gas drift away, leaving behind a white-hot core called a **white dwarf**. It lights up the surrounding cloud of dust and gas. This stardust can eventually form new stars and planets.

An artist's impression of a white dwarf star system. Someday our sun will become a white dwarf.

This artist's impression shows a yellow dwarf like our sun in the foreground. The blue star behind it is eight times more massive than the sun, and the darker blue star in the background is three hundred times more massive.

The life span of any star depends on its size. The biggest and hottest stars burn their fuel quickly and last only a few million years. Smaller stars consume fuel slowly and can burn for billions of years. Our sun is about five billion years old and is expected to last for another five billion years.

GaLaXIes

On a clear night, away from the lights of a city, you may see a faint band of light arcing across the sky. The light is from thousands and thousands of stars. From Earth, we can see just a tiny portion of the stars in the Milky Way.

Without the aid of a telescope, all the stars you can see in the night sky are in the Milky Way.

A galaxy is a huge cluster of stars, gas, and dust held together by gravity. A galaxy may have millions or billions of stars. The Milky Way has about one hundred billion stars.

Scientists think most galaxies have a supermassive black hole at their center that may have formed by many smaller black holes combining. In 2018 scientists used telescopes to confirm the black hole at the center of the Milky Way. Thousands of other black holes may surround it.

In 2019 scientists released this image of the black hole at the center of the Messier 87 galaxy.

A UNIVERSE OF GALAXIES

Galaxies come in many shapes. The Milky Way is spiral-shaped, with curved arms like a pinwheel. Some galaxies look like ovals, others like toothpicks or even blobs.

Everything in the Milky Way orbits the supermassive black hole at the galaxy's center, Sagittarius A*.

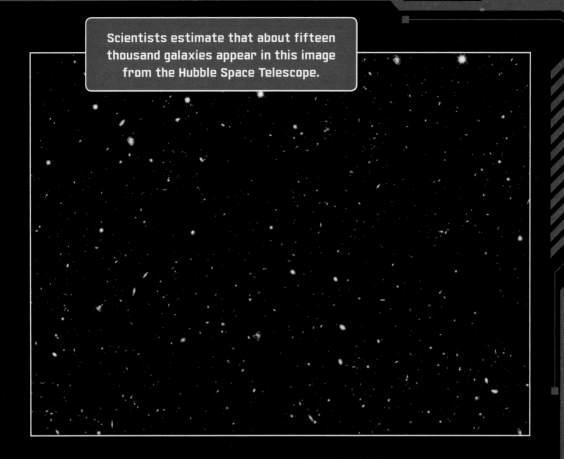
Scientists estimate that about fifteen thousand galaxies appear in this image from the Hubble Space Telescope.

There are so many galaxies in the universe that astronomers haven't counted them all. The Hubble Space Telescope looked deeply at one patch of space and found thousands of galaxies. Astronomers think there could be as many as one hundred billion galaxies in the universe.

Sometimes two galaxies smash together and form a new galaxy. The Milky Way could someday collide with our nearest neighbor, the Andromeda galaxy. But that won't happen for billions of years.

TIME TRAVEL

Looking at stars and galaxies from Earth is like looking back in time. That's because light from space takes time to reach Earth. Light moves about 186,000 miles (299,337 km) per second. Light from the sun takes more than eight minutes to reach us. So when you look at the sun, you see it as it looked more than eight minutes ago.

The shape and color of galaxies can tell scientists about their age and how they formed.

Andromeda galaxy

Andromeda is the nearest spiral-shaped galaxy to the Milky Way.

Light from more distant stars takes longer to reach Earth. You see Alpha Centauri, the next-nearest star system, as it looked more than four years ago. When you look at other galaxies, you are looking even further back in time because they are farther from Earth. You see Andromeda as it looked 2.5 million years ago.

In 2016 Hubble took this image of galaxy GN-z11 (*inset*). The picture captures the galaxy as it looked 13.4 billion years ago when the universe was just 3 percent of its current age.

By looking farther and deeper into space, telescopes have allowed us to see further back in time. Hubble has looked at galaxies as they existed more than thirteen billion years ago. Astronomers are studying these images to learn what the early universe was like.

Astronomers hope to keep looking further into the past. The James Webb Space Telescope is a new, superpowered telescope designed to see farther and deeper into space than ever before. It is scheduled to launch in 2021. What secrets of stars and galaxies will it reveal?

The James Webb Space Telescope will orbit Earth almost 1 million miles (1.6 million km) above the planet.

Follow the links below to download 3D printer files for a nebula and two of the telescopes in this book:

Hubble Space Telescope, http://qrs.lernerbooks.com/Hubble

James Webb Space Telescope, http://qrs.lernerbooks.com/JamesWebb

Eta Carinae Homunculus Nebula, http://qrs.lernerbooks.com /EtaCarinae

atmosphere: gases surrounding a planet or a star

atoms: tiny particles of matter

auroras: displays of light in the sky that occur near Earth's North Pole and South Pole

black hole: a dense area of space with very strong gravity. A black hole forms when a large star collapses.

chain reaction: a nuclear reaction producing energy that causes even more nuclear reactions

charged particles: very small bits of matter with an electric charge

fusion: the joining of atoms to form heavier atoms. Fusion releases enormous amounts of energy.

mass: the amount of matter in an object

orbits: moves in a path around a body in space

supernova: the violent explosion of a very large star

white dwarf: a dying star that is small, dense, and not very bright

FURTHER INFORMATION

DK. *Space! The Universe as You've Never Seen It Before*. New York: DK, 2015.

European Space Agency: Star Birth
https://www.esa.int/kids/en/learn/Our_Universe/Stars_and _galaxies/Star_birth

NASA Space Place: Sun
https://spaceplace.nasa.gov/menu/sun/

NASA: What Is a Supernova?
https://www.nasa.gov/audience/forstudents/5-8/features/nasa -knows/what-is-a-supernova.html

Peterson, Christy. *Breakthroughs in Stars Research*. Minneapolis: Lerner Publications, 2019.

Roland, James. *Black Holes: A Space Discovery Guide*. Minneapolis: Lerner Publications, 2017.

Schneider, Howard. *Night Sky*. Washington, DC: National Geographic, 2016.

Stars
https://starchild.gsfc.nasa.gov/docs/StarChild/universe_level2 /stars.html

Photo Acknowledgments

Image credits: Freer/Shutterstock.com, p. 2 (bottom); NASA/Solar Dynamics Observatory (CC BY 2.0), p. 4; NASA/JPL-Caltech, pp. 5, 25; NASA/NRL/Parker Solar Probe, p. 6; NASA/Parker Solar Probe, p. 7; Laura Westlund/Independent Picture Service, p. 8; NASA/SDO, pp. 9, 10; Ekaterina Kondratova/Shutterstock.com, p. 11; NASA, ESA and Allison Loll/Jeff Hester (Arizona State University), Davide De Martin (ESA/Hubble), p. 12; NASA/JPL-Caltech/R. Hurt (SSC), p. 13; ESO, p. 14; ESA/Hubble and Digitized Sky Survey 2, Davide De Martin (ESA/Hubble), p. 15; NASA, ESA, A. Goobar (Stockholm University), and the Hubble Heritage Team (STScI/AURA), p. 16; Peter Garnavich, Harvard-Smithsonian Center for Astrophysics, the High-z Supernova Search Team, and NASA/ESA, p. 17; NASA, ESA, and Z. Levy (STScI), p. 18; ESO/M. Kornmesser, p. 19; ESO/B. Tafreshi (twanight.org), p. 20; Event Horizon Telescope Collaboration (CC BY 3.0), p. 21; Alex Mit/Shutterstock.com, p. 22; NASA, ESA, P. Oesch (University of Geneva), and M. Montes (University of New South Wales), p. 23; Robert Williams and the Hubble Deep Field Team (STScI) and NASA/ESA, p. 24; NASA, ESA, and P. Oesch (Yale University), p. 26; NASA/Goddard Space Flight Center (CC BY 2.0), p. 27; Bob Wick, BLM/flickr (CC BY 2.0), p. 28. Design elements: Jetrel/Shutterstock.com; Nanashiro/Shutterstock.com; phiseksit/Shutterstock.com; MSSA/Shutterstock.com; Pakpoom Makpan/Shutterstock.com; pixelparticle/Shutterstock.com; wacomka/Shutterstock.com; fluidworkshop/Shutterstock.com.

Cover: Alex Mit/Shutterstock.com.

Copyright © 2020 by Lerner Publishing Group, Inc.

All rights reserved. International copyright secured. No part of this book may be reproduced, stored in a retrieval system, or transmitted in any form or by any means—electronic, mechanical, photocopying, recording, or otherwise—without the prior written permission of Lerner Publishing Group, Inc., except for the inclusion of brief quotations in an acknowledged review.

Lerner Publications Company
An imprint of Lerner Publishing Group, Inc.
241 First Avenue North
Minneapolis, MN USA 55401

For reading levels and more information, look up this title at www.lernerbooks.com.

Main body text set in Aptifer Sans LT Pro.
Typeface provided by Linotype AG.

Library of Congress Cataloging-in-Publication Data

Names: Hirsch, Rebecca E., author.
Title: Stars and galaxies in action : an augmented reality experience / Rebecca E.
    Hirsch.
Description: Minneapolis : Lerner Publications, [2020] | Series: Space exploration
    (Alternator books) | Audience: Ages 8–12. | Audience: Grades 4 to 6.
Identifiers: LCCN 2019014591 (print) | LCCN 2019018507 (ebook) |
    ISBN 9781541583535 (eb pdf) | ISBN 9781541578791 (lb : alk. paper)
Subjects: LCSH: Stars—Evolution—Juvenile literature. | Stars—Juvenile literature. |
    Galaxies—Evolution—Juvenile literature. | Galaxies—Juvenile literature.
Classification: LCC QB806 (ebook) | LCC QB806 .H57 2020 (print) | DDC 523—dc23

LC record available at https://lccn.loc.gov/2019014591

Manufactured in the United States of America
1-46982-47851-7/3/2019